the space that connects us

the
space
that
connects
us

poems

Mansa Trotman

©2012 Mansa Trotman

Except for purposes of review, no part of this book may be reproduced in any form without prior permission of the publisher.

We acknowledge the support of the Canada Council for the Arts for our publishing program. We also acknowledge support from the Government of Ontario through the Ontario Arts Council.

We acknowledge the financial support of the Government of Canada through the Canada Book Fund for our publishing activities.

  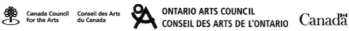

Cover design by Christa Seeley

Library and Archives Canada Cataloguing in Publication

Trotman, Mansa,
    The space that connects us : poems / Mansa Trotman.

ISBN 978-1-894770-95-8

    I. Title.

PS8639.R649S63 2012   C811'.6   C2012-905430-5

Printed and bound in Canada by Coach House Printing

TSAR Publications
P. O. Box 6996, Station A
Toronto, Ontario M5W 1X7
Canada

www.tsarbooks.com

Contents

Aria in the Key of You 1
The Space that Connects Us 2
Counting Changes 3
Untitled 4
Unholy Trinity 6
Touching Bone 8
Widowed 9
July 27th 10
Men Like You 12
Butterfly Kisses 13
Judy Blume Diary (in fragments) 14
Nocturnal Melodies 16
Cartography 18
Untitled 20
Untitled 21
3-(x)= 22
Lineage 23
Untitled 24
And Look What the Future Has Wrought 25
Mama 28
The MRS 30
The Block 32
Untitled 33
Tara and Roberto 34
Have You Ever Fallen in Love Just Because It Was Counterintuitive 35
Marrow 36
A Poem of Life 37
Back Home Days 38
Defiance 39
In Sleeping With Anger 41
Raw Writing 43

Silk Satin And Cotton 44
The Art of Possession 45
When I Was Real 47
Without You 49
I Was Perfectly Fine 50
Netting 51

Aria in the Key of You

i am bewitched by your name and the sound it makes in my
throat
sometimes it is a melody that i am glad to be comforted by
i stroke your name with my voice i roll it around on my
tongue i slowly kiss it
goodnight
and allow it to rock me to sleep
sometimes it awakens me as a scream and
it scrapes my throat and tongue

it bangs into my teeth and squeezes itself through pursed lips
i am as tired of the goodness your name brings to me as i am
with the nightmares
and
when i fall asleep with the taste of your name on my lips
it is a bitter hue
i am then reminded that the taste of you has always been a
conflict in tenses, senses and
character
you are at once my sweet lullaby – your name rocks my soul to
sleep
and my bitter tranquilizer   colouring my
dreams tasteless
i am a study in contradiction
looking always for slumber in the key of you

The Space that Connects Us

i find our connection in such a tiny yet important place
it is akin to the space that connects hand to forearm, foot to shin, knuckle to
fingertip
        it is a joint
and in the minute space that connects us
a multitude of poetry can be written in fluid script
and now it is the words that connect us in that small space
and i lick them up when they drip
so that i might be able to connect to you with speech

Counting Changes

I count the pennies and you the dimes
In the middle of the living room floor
Where we once danced
The clock ticks away from the dream
We had put a mortgage on
And neglected payments
I count the minutes now and
Wonder if we will ever go back to the times
When we used to lay
Half on the bed   half off
Nude
Drinking orange juice out of wine glasses
And pretending it was champagne
Wondering how we were gonna spend the rest
Of our lives if we couldn't even figure out the next hour
When all I had to do, all I really wanted to do
Was (kiss) (hold) (taste)
You
Eat the essence of you
Stapled my lips shut
So that a drop dare not drip
My fingertips rolled down your spine
As we danced
And yours drummed my back slightly to the beat
But now my fingertips count pennies and yours dimes
And the living room holds us hostage without music.

Untitled

I put my trust into his hand and tell him "make a fist to keep it locked there"
Make a fist and keep it locked there but her breath blows in his ears,
On his neck and on his fist
Her breath blows across miles and
He is powerless to her strength and his fist opens and my trust leaks
Slowly down his arm
He does not care enough to even lick a few drops up
I am dripping down toward his elbow and he is looking out towards her
Strength
She is strength because to him she is perfection
Perfect in her looks her intelligence and even more perfect in her
Distance
The closer you come to someone the more flaws are visible
With distance she gives him the gift of illusion, the gift of non-commitment
I have nothing like this to offer   my trust is all I had
And now it is gone
Allowed to drain from his hand
Without so much as a lick
He bathes me in words his words that spiral around my naked body
I am mesmerized by these words and I allow them to moisturize me
He is becoming my strength
I stand before him dressed in yet another frock of sadness
But his head is turned looking for more strength

Mop up my trust and put it back in your hand I say
Put fist to heart for safekeeping
I go back for more and each time his fist opens and closes
There is less of me to fit in my wardrobe of disappointment
His arm, sticky with traces of trust reaches
Out to her but she is too far
And it is only then that I realize that we are in the same predicament
He has used my faith as fuel   I have used his words
And what a sight we make
Me in a patchwork dress of heartache
And him with wet arm outstretched
Reaching away from the truth he has always known

Unholy Trinity

this unholy trinity
this man woman woman triangle that we subscribe to
this she gets you this week and I the next
affair
this cell phone, home phone, leave a message cause I'm with
her kind of deal
this measuring up game I play with her
and she doesn't even know my name
this unknowing competition we have
all refereed by you
this don't kiss me on my cheek cause someone might know
just give me a pound in the club so that no one suspects kind
of flex
it is a silly situation, but it is an all-too-familiar mode of
operation
and
don't make me feel like I'm the other woman cause she is just
as much the other as I
we are the same woman halved
we are the same woman she gets you this week and I the next
and don't make me act like I am a mistress in your deceit
she is just as much your mistress as I
she knows only half and I the other
we take turns
and I know it is not her week when you call me more than
once
she sits at home
she sits at home and leaves a message
you're with me it's that kind of deal
it is a silent deal you make with both of us separately
this secret, down-low affair

this defective booty call
this booty call on crack
and this week she sits at home knowing that even though she
played by all the rules
she has been moved to another degree of the triangle
and I now sit to the right
in this unholy trinity
lover, his girl and his girl this week
AMEN

Touching Bone

It waits like a flashback
Like moving images flitting
Across my eyes
I touched your hip with my fingertips and I melted into it
Touched Bone
Looked up at the ceiling, counted cracks
If I dared look into your eyes
I would be lost, drowned
Nothing was safe anymore
No more home base when you moved in with all your baggage
And I allowed you to unpack in my womb
Beckoned you to my life, my world, with words – with hands
and lips, teeth, tongue played down your spine
You kissed me until you cried
And I held you, slid into you
Touched Bone
Eyes now grabbed onto the ceiling
It was solid, it was keeping me sane
Would not let me fall
So you fell into me instead
Melted sweet chocolate
Touched Bone

Widowed

Struck down like this
Time measured in breaths
Sleep coming in waves
Hanging on by navel strings
A different kind of death
A waiting game of sorts
I am holding my own hand
I am stroking my own feet
I am loving my own self
And it is not something I am used to
Not accustomed to being alone
I want to look for someone to be mad at
To blame this on
But all that is left
Is time
Which falters now
And sleep whose waters
Have stilled

July 27th

It was happening and when it was happening I said
This doesn't feel real
This couldn't be real
This isn't real and so it wasn't 'cause I wished it
To another place
 And when I looked down at you
You were someone else
You were not here but your eyes were closed and your
Mouth was open
And I think you let sound escape
But I couldn't hear it above mine
I was trying not to let myself hear so it wouldn't become
Real
So it wouldn't be happening
And I let you come inside me
Half because it seemed natural and
Half because I wanted to see
What you would do what you would say
If you would move out of me if you would look up at me
If I would hear sound
But the air was silent
And it was stifling enough to let me realize you were not
Kissing me
You had not kissed me
I did not know what your lips tasted like
What they felt like
If they were soft like your hands that brushed by me on
Their way up to hold the bedpost
Those lips I could see being licked by tongue
I did not know if they were rough like the blanket you
Lay on when I lay on you

I remember thinking I wanted to write poetry about
Those lips
About things that I could see but could not touch
About things that I could see but not know
I wanted to write poetry about the way it felt to not
Be loved by you
I wanted to write from memory and use my daydreams
As notes
I wanted to write pretty words hoping you would
Mistake them for me
You didn't understand me any better than you
Understood those words
To you
poetry was a mystery
But I remember thinking if I only could show you that
This was poetry
That every movement we made separately or
Together was poetry
That you were poetry
Maybe you could understand and
I tried to catch every word that floated in the air with us
Hoping I could put them together later
Put them together to show you how beautiful poetry
Could be
To show you how beautiful we could be

Men Like You

Don't exist save for movies and poetry like mine
You with the fluid lines of chocolate limbs
Glide into my life and saturate my mind
I am addicted to the taste of your voice
Attracted to the texture of your smile
I touch your lips with my fingertips and close my eyes
Believing
That it belongs to me
But men like you don't exist save for old movies
And longing poetry
Like mine
So I will have to write daily to keep you around

Butterfly Kisses

Back in those days
when you lay on my chest
and I stroked your head where the hair no longer grew
your eyelashes brushed my skin making butterfly prayers on
my breast
and I had no idea that I would
end up here in these days
thinking I wasted my love and life on you
I used to dream in movies
romantic tales with vaseline glazed lenses
so it is no wonder I expected you to be my prince charming
believed that you would be the hero in my script
but life is not a cinderella fairy tale
with creamy celluloid plots
and I know now
that those butterfly prayers were not a promise of a happy
ending
but instead just your eyes closing in sleep
as I rubbed your head where the hair no longer grows

Judy Blume Diary (in fragments)

when I remember the
first times
I don't see me I see hair
with too much hair grease
I see shoulders and a bedroom door
over the horizon

they are always the first times
it is what I tell them and
what I tell myself
they are my first times because it hasn't been love yet
it is sweaty palms, shakily rolling down the condom
half-hoping he won't have to wear it
it is guinea-pig sex
it is
"let's see if she'll do it in the back of a schoolyard
let's see if she'll do it on her bathroom floor"
kind of sex
and she does
it is never really me

and in the diaries
from my teenage years
I see fragments of me
or impressions of me left in the memory of it
me topless, headless
modeling for him/them
parading in a hotel room
and all the time
wondering if my skin needed cream
me without arms

cause I didn't want to feel his hairy chest
I am stroking his collarbone with
the stumps where my shoulders should be
me with no legs
cause he stretched them too far
to see them would bring back the pain.

Nocturnal Melodies

There was no start to this, it has always been. I dreamed you as poetry so that I could know you. I dreamed you as poetry that I could know myself. I dreamed you as a heart with all valves open. I dreamed you as music and you were the blues. I dreamed in colour and you were black. I dreamed experimentally with words as characters.

you were life   endless strength   endless life were you

I believed in the dream. You were so close, you felt so real. When at last you saw me, recognition stood still in your eyes. You were my dream and you remembered.

And when we first danced and I went home with your scent staining my clothes I knew I wanted to smell you again. I wanted to become liquid in your arms and fall from you in a steady stream. I wanted to smell like you.

You sipped my body like it was music. I licked sweat expecting sweetness. I found salt. You said fucking was like eating good food. I didn't know what you meant. You said I just needed more practice. I whispered your name as a mantra and you asked me to come with you; I held you and said anywhere, you just laughed.

And when you kissed me there was only tongue, snake-sliding no-mouth-smile and you told me you could teach me how. To tongue you, to slide with no mouth was to kiss with no smile. I wanted to know your jewels but you asked if I was a gold digger or a ball-breaker; you didn't understand.

When I was alone and lonely I wished you here and you reappeared in the music just below the bass calling my name, haunting my space and I was glad. We went back to the dance with me in my aloneliness and you riding the bass, but the song stained me this time.

I wished you back from that realm rewinding over and over but it seemed that you were lost, deciding between Melody and Harmony not sure if they were the same. I wished that I were somewhere in the middle of those two. I wished I were the number left behind when they were subtracted. I wished I were difference. I wished you mine.

Once in a prelude to kissing you, I bit your bottom lip then said that I loved you. There was silence in the moment before you asked me why. That was an easy question and I listed the reasons. I listed my dreams. I listed the wishes that I had swallowed whole as if they were truth. I listed you. You looked through me and then said that I had my heart in the wrong part, that this wasn't love and never had been. I thought I had heard that in a song somewhere but I couldn't quite catch the echo.

I told you that this was the stuff good writing was made of. You said you weren't sure what I meant. I started to say you just needed . . . You finished with practice. I smiled. If writing was to come of this, you said, then how would I write it? I said I would write it as poetry, as the blues in black. I said I would experiment in writing dreams from an open heart. I said I would write you.

Cartography

I dreamed you the other night. It was almost the same dream I had before I met you except this time you had a face. You were running toward me. I was surrounded by people but I could still see you and you were running toward me. At one point in the dream we locked eyes; yours were just as black as they are in real life and they were looking through me. It was as if there was another me behind me and you were running to her cause you didn't see me. You kept running and the wall parted for you and just as we were about to collide I woke up so I didn't get to see if you found the other me. I reached for you because I forgot that you had left. My hand hit the wall.

Did you dream me last night? I always believed when I was younger that people in love dreamed the same dreams. Did you dream me? Were you running toward me or were you running away?

It's funny how you just left. There wasn't really a fight or a discussion, one day you said you were leaving and I said goodbye and that was that. Maybe we had the discussions in our heads. But it has been almost a year and I still cook for two. I still watch TV until 3 AM waiting for you to call for me. I still reach for you in bed. Maybe I didn't mean good-bye. Maybe I was wrong.

I sleep with a light on now so that I can find my way in the dark. Without you there, my inner map has been screwed up and I seem to stumble on my way to the bathroom. Besides, I am not used to the noises this house makes when there is no laughter in it. It moans and it scares me. And it talks to me in a language I haven't quite grasped yet. I have time, I will learn. I think it misses you too. Or rather, it misses us.

Tonight I had a bubble bath for old times' sake and in the robe that you bought me two birthdays ago I sat up and tried to speak to this house. I told it my dreams and my fears. I talked to it like I would have talked to you. And then I wrote you my heart because you always said you wanted it.

Untitled

i loved me my whole life until I met you
and then there was no longer any me to love
i was not me once you moved into my skin
and i became the shell

i loved me my whole entire life and then i met you
and you became my story
everything you did or said became engraved on my skin
injustices imprinted on my breasts and back

i loved me, all of me, in entirety before i met you
and since then it has been a slow and steady crawl back to
where i began
i'm not there yet but i'm on my way, i haven't arrived yet but
i'm getting there
when i will love me regardless of who you are

Untitled

Last night I thought
I might cry until
My heart bled empty

It was different than
the time my crush
went unrequited and
I thought I might die
from the weight
different too than the
time I thought
I might cry my eyes
dry from loneliness

Last night I thought
I might cry until
my heart bled empty
and it was different
than the time my love
loved another and I wanted
to jump but couldn't see
the ledge through the tears

This cry last night was
different because it was
my cry for me
a cry for my wisdom
and my pain
a cry for my heart,
still beating still taking
care of me and still full with an unending
capacity to love

3-(x)=

Subtract me from
This equation
Count me out because
I can no longer
Be the lonely letter in brackets
Life defined by the actions of you
Subtract me because
I want to be difference

Lineage

I see her often in my dreams. She has your smile only hers still resides in her eyes. She moves like you do and I find myself falling in love with you when I hear her laugh.
I have wanted her for so long. I am pregnant with the idea of what she will become. I have wanted her longer than I have known you and yet I have always known that she would be yours.
I want you to teach her your world so that she can always have the self-confidence I have yearned for.
Your world builds survivors. Self-sufficient, strong. I want her to know that. I want her to be fathered by you.
My world makes dreamers. Hopeful, optimistic. I want her to know that too. I want her to be mothered by me.
Nurtured by both of us. The best of both worlds.
But I want her to know that even in your world you had poetry, dreamed of what you could become.
And in my world I endured pain, survived the battle I have scars as memories.
That is how we come together.
Two lives, like experiences, coming together to raise this girl-child into a woman.

Untitled

suffering is hot.
and sticky
it clings to skin and clothes
its scent lingers
the humility of it all
the humidity of it all
i know it well

And Look What the Future Has Wrought

bobbed
pixie
shoulder-length
braid it, French and Congo, are really the same
extend it, synthetically
brush it 50 times not a stroke less
spray it
activate it
oil-sheen it
hot-comb it
chemically treat it
straighten it
perm it
texturize it
relax it (gently of course)
more like fry it
is it burning?
don't scratch
try to ignore the smell
highlight it
rinse it
dye it
permanently colour it
'til it grows out
spiral-curl it
dry it with a hand-held spray of hot air
moisturize it
cover it with a plastic cap
pull it back
tease it
frizz it
mousse it

gel it
hair-spray it
make sure it has extra hold
holds like glue
so the curls won't droop
the style won't fade
head-band it so the roots won't show
or if it's been more than two months
you're best to cover it
or use the old trick
of handfuls of Vaseline and blow dryer
damage
breakage
split ends
conditioning treatments
olive oil and mayonnaise
placenta
super-grow formula
natural herbs and
steam treatments
because we can't deviate from the norm
gotta have long, straight hair
for him to run his hands through and not get stuck
it's gotta have bounce
it's gotta have body
can't look like a duplicate of him
gotta look like a woman with
hair that swings when you walk
hair that moves when you laugh
hair that he can run his hands through and not get stuck
so what will us women do next?
in our bid to maintain the norm, we really did deviate
because the norm before us, before our mothers, actually it was

before their mothers
was kinky hair
thick hair
hair that didn't have to swing
hair that didn't have to move
hair that didn't have to have a hand go through it, unstuck
to validate its worth

Mama

Mama sits down
'cause tired bones grow
weary in the evening
She gotta think
'cause there only
a few days left
till all those bills gotta be paid
one more night with Mr Man
would surely kill her
but them bills gotta be paid
somehow
she gotta find a way
to get those pills
she could take
'cause there ain't no more
room for those babies she make
when Mr Man
too drunk to remember his promise or even care

This is what love come down to
the bridge between
money and the bills
a heart can only take
so much
but Mama gotta push hers to the limit
else them kids gonna go
like those others
only a few and who's countin'?
she is – backward from a hundred
then it be all over
supposed to be but she still remember

the time she started from 79
and saw it all
when she was supposed to be
sleepin the pain away
it meant that extra bill
never surfaced

but sometimes Mama gotta close her eyes
squeeze em shut
hold her hands over her ears
till them memories fly away up there
hangin on to angel wings
till that angel and her
get a chance to meet again
and she did it
three times – as if to see if she was
tough enough to really handle it
but Mama always can
she ain't built on stilts
the hard concrete's what keeping her
firm on the ground
with a plan in her head
and that man seem to be it
so she picks up the phone to see what he up to

The MRS

The phone is ringing
Again
But the Mrs ain't gonna answer
It
It's for him again she know for sure
And she too tired to deal with those whores
Her Mr Like to deal with
He come home
To their home
Late at night and he stale-drunk
And when she tell him of her new finding
He says he's sorry
'Cause he never gave that woman the number
She must have looked it up
The Mrs Sure he have kids out there
'Cause she saw one
Look just like him in the market last Saturday
The skin was lighter but them eyes
Was the same
And that nose and lips couldn't
Belong to anyone else
But she don't get shocked no more
Disbelief is a waste nowadays
'Cause any and everything is
Possible
Like those diseases she keep getting
And no matter what the good doctor do
Can't make it go away forever
'Cause those women still be there
The first time
She was shocked

But by the fifth
She had grown into this cloak
Of denial that had once been many sizes too big
But she stays cause she ain't going out like her Mama did
In the back alley of life
Hopin the pain would go away
The Mrs Just waitin
He don't touch her no more
So she don't have to shirk his advances
But she just waitin for him to die.

The Block

i can't write anymore.
i don't remember how.
the words won't come
they stay in the incubator of my womb
comfortable in their embryonic state

Untitled

my heart is breaking
when he sounds rushed, annoyed, disinterested
a rip tears down the centre
my heart is breaking
it is tired, overused, abused by others
unsoothed, neglected and malnourished by me
my heart is breaking
and I have no tools to fix it

Tara and Roberto

hola mi amor
those were the first words
i heard her speak to him
eyelashes fluttering like their hearts
like butterfly wings
their words spanned across miles
acting as a bridge
connecting these lives
combining two cultures
two families
dos corazones
hola mi esposa

Have You Ever Fallen in Love Just Because It Was Counterintuitive

or scrambled for pen in sleep hoping to catch the words before they buried into pillow
written poems on backs of pay stubs stuffed in the bottoms of overpriced handbags
saved them in draft folders wondering if your life would forever be a draft; just practice
waiting to press send
spent hours pondering the importance of a comma, capital letter or period
while buying baby clothes in anticipation of conception

Marrow

There is no more love to be drained from these bones
You have sucked the marrow dry
And nothing is left save for three beads of sweat
On foreheads where kisses were once laid to rest

A Poem of Life

I want to write a poem about my uterus
Doctors want to tell me that it's tipped the wrong way
They decide when to take a growth out
and when it's "safe" to keep it in
They seem to know more about my uterus and me
Than I do
Macho men want to damage it with harsh symbolic tones
of manhood
Maybe if they bang it hard enough all of my feminine
strength will
dissolve in a pool at their feet

This is a poem about my uterus
You should know that place where pro-lifers say you should
store
the next mass murderer
even if you want to take it out?
That mysterious place that I hardly know how to spell let
alone say
'cause teachers are too embarrassed to tell me about it

This is a poem for my uterus
I hardly know if it's mine anymore.

Back Home Days

I like to eat good food.
There's nothing like a big, fat roti with the
juices running freely when you take a bite
A real man's meal
And everything is nice, nice.

I like a good drink too.
Gimme a cold Carib from de fridge
No glass necessary
just give it to me straight like that.
Then everyting is nice, nice.

Then I could take a sleep.
Dream 'bout Rosie with her round bottom rolling
in time to de Kaiso
All de men and dem would be wishing they were me.
An Rosie smiling, 'cause she know is me she
coming home wid.
And everyting would be nice, nice.

Defiance

I am one
classified as one of them (all)
classified in terms of what I'm not
of what limits me (supposedly)
I am one
Somehow qualified to speak
the feelings of politicians, leaders,
criminals, friends, ancestors
(because, of course, they're all the same)
but I'm me
What will you call me?
non-white (what?)
visible minority (invisible?)
black, brown, coloured
(don't miss a spot – don't go outside the lines!)
light-skinned, dark-skinned
boxed and packaged, cut and scraped
until I fit a mould
That calms you
makes you feel
comfortable
Don't worry, you're using the right term this week
Until it
(or I)
no longer fit
Outgrew that one
Think of something else
I left that one behind as well
And you have to catch me now 'cause
I'm flying
over lumps and clumps of your classifications

Look closely and you'll find people
real people who you lumped
and clumped together from the beginning
You called them a different name
Gave them a different term
but they're still here
Can't classify them into oblivion
Can't limit them until they can't think
We will still be here defying classifications.

In Sleeping with Anger

In sleeping with anger
I have learned to use
the shape of words
the sound of thought
to communicate
through windows, doors
chains and gates
that held me captured
– at times enraptured –
with eyes that glisten
smile of the wicked

In sleeping with anger
I have tried to grow used to
the bruises
that scream for help
– been shocked seeing them on my own skin –
So many
they make a design
Map my back
thighs
neck

Myriad circumstances, stories told
this one – for the time we talked too soon
this one – for the time we talked too late and that one
that one's for the time we loved too much

But

in sleeping with anger

I have grown strong enough to learn
that in sleeping with anger
you are sleeping with the enemy

Beware

Raw Writing

As if it is to be cooked
Boiled, fried, baked
To be eaten by the ones who devour poetry
Without understanding its meaning
As if it would taste good without
Time to stew, marinate
Sit in creative juices
And then heat in ovens of the mind
I want my writing steamed
Just enough to be palatable
Not overcooked to the point that it is tough and takes
Too long to chew

Silk Satin And Cotton

How do I compete?
She of flesh and I merely of fabric
he can whisper and she respond
I can only listen
She smooth with sweat
and I crinkle with the freshness of waiting for a few drops
to drip
I am always left with
the residue of their passion
the proof of their lust
They throw me in the washer
to hide it

The Art of Possession

He had silky hair he used to touch when he talked to me. I was more aware of my looks when I looked at him. I didn't feel good enough in his light. Covered up imperfections until I was covering up bruises.

I met him at a mall in his cool clothes and with his smooth lyrics he convinced me that he was the one for me. I believed and fell into the trap that he set. My outer layers were eventually cut off and in my flesh were big hunkering bites.

Some looked disapprovingly as if that would make a difference. And some almost stopped and some tried to ask if I was alright. But he shooed them away with his slick talk. The same talk he used to reel me in. Words seemed to slide off his tongue. Words seemed to wrap around my throat. And I was almost more afraid of his tongue and words than I was of his hands; his fists.

Contradicting hands – used to hold me, caress me – same hands used to grip me and then beat me. He took my breath away with his looks, his punches. He made me laugh with his jokes 'til I cried from his kicks. And then he bore into me with his dick.
His dick felt much like his eyes with which he tore into my soul; it turned me to brittle bone – I still have the cracks to prove it. And yet my hips welcomed him. The more I loved him the more he owned me.

My legs, my breasts, my body were his. And I felt like a slate – that he could create on – that he could design and manufacture – that he could put out for the world to see.

And sometimes it wasn't so blatant. And sometimes it wasn't out in the open. He used communication like a knife. Slicing into me with his silence and then picking up the pieces of me with new words of affection, of love.

Love was his game that he mastered like a pro and I played by the rules. He changed them at the drop of a hat. He governed the way I looked, the way I dressed, even the colour toenail polish I wore. And I followed them to please him. I followed them for his approval.

I tell you that before you ask. I tell you that 'cause people ask the questions. The same people who almost stopped. They ask questions in their comfy offices, from their comfy lives. And I have a simple answer that they seem not to understand. But nothing could be simpler than love.

And I sit here with his baby swimming in my belly and him miles away with his new catch. Ad I hope that it will not be a boy 'cause I would surely die if I had to raise another him. I sit with his baby swimming in my belly and I hope that it will not be a girl 'cause I wouldn't want to raise another me.

When I Was Real

Had I been a real woman
maybe I would have run
with open arms to you
Might have smiled while you called me
Sugar, baby, honey, schnookie even
Might have blushed when you told me
how tasty I looked
Ready for you to take a bite
But I couldn't bear the thought
of seeing myself on yet another menu

And so I was reduced to being called a bitch
A cop-out is what that is
To you every woman is a bitch
first 'cause she's out for the money
then 'cause she's out for the fame
Maybe just 'cause she's out
She's a woman
No explanation needed
Some kind of weak sex, fragile
Praised only when she has to act
more like a man
Rough and Ready
to somehow turn into a real woman
A high-heel wearing, stand-by-her-man,
real woman
A real woman with false lashes and inches of makeup trying to hide
the fact that she's
Desperate for your real man love
Paranoid someone else might get your superlatives

In all their splendour
An instant mommy to you and all the kids you'll "give" me
I'll "give" you
Which is politically correct in "Real Woman Land"?
I would rather be a real woman working to pay more than
just the daycare and diaper bills
doing more than just mothering you
I love you but I didn't carry you for nine months
and I'm not gonna carry you for the rest of my life
I love you but I don't seem real enough for you
With my arms wide open I would run to you
But I can't see through these lashes and
I'm afraid I might break a heel.

Without You

Had a gourmet dinner
last night without you

Ate every last bite
and licked my fingers
just to prove that
I did it without you

No fireworks, loud noise or congratulations
I just did it
and tomorrow after work
I'm gonna do it again.

I Was Perfectly Fine

i was perfectly fine where you found me. life carved out in slippery stone . . . love eked out in measures . . . i was perfectly fine
and you came and made clay of my stone

Netting

We have come undone
The tight coil of lies and deceit we
So carefully wound
Unraveled under a number of feet

What once held us together
Untethered, unglued
By truth

I wanted you to read me
To know my every biographical line
Until I found that fairy tales were easier
That you smiled more when I was masked

I chased that smile
Used lies as my net
Reeled you in . . . winding wool over your eyes

But nets only last so long
Before frayed strings are pulled
And fish are flit-flitting back to sea

We have come undone
Unwound, untethered, unglued

Uncoiled by truth.